WRITTEN BY

What Sarah Did Next

© CWR 2020
Published 2020 by CWR, Waverley Abbey House, Waverley Lane, Farnham,
Surrey GU9 8EP, UK
Tel: 01252 784700 Email: mail@cwr.org.uk Registered Charity No. 294387
Registered Limited Company No. 1990308

Unless otherwise indicated, all Scripture references are from The Holy Bible,
New International Version (Anglicised edition), copyright © 1979, 1984,
2011 by Biblica (formerly International Bible Society).
Concept development, editing, design and production by CWR.
Front cover image: AdobeStock/kichigin19
Printed in the UK by Linney.

MIX
Paper from
responsible sources
FSC® C015900

How to get the best out of *Life Every Day*

HERE ARE A FEW SUGGESTIONS:

- Ideally, carve out a regular time and place each day, with as few distractions as possible. Ask God what He has to say to you.

- Read the Bible passages suggested in the 'Read' references. (As tempting as it is, try not to skip the Bible reading and get straight into the notes.)

- The 'Focus' reference then gives you one or two verses to look at in more detail. Consider what the reading is saying to you and what challenges that may bring.

- Each day's comments are part of an overall theme. Try to recall what you read the previous day so that you maintain a sense of continuity.

- Spend time thinking about how to apply what God has said to you. Ask Him to help you do this.

- Pray the prayer at the end as if it were your own. Perhaps add your own prayer in response to what you have read and been thinking about.

Join in the conversation on Facebook
facebook.com/jefflucasuk

A tangled family background

Read:
Joshua 24:2–4
1 Corinthians
1:26–31

It is around four thousand years ago. A rather dysfunctional family, where men marry their half-sisters, is living in a thriving ancient city called Ur (the ruins of which are found in modern Iraq). They are moon worshippers, and their names reflect their devotion to their occult practices. Their dark religion includes human sacrifice, and the city is dominated by a massive, three-staged ziggurat building. It was to this family that God came, calling them to be planet changers. We still experience the massive reverberations of their decisions all these years later. This was Abraham and Sarah. To be specific, they shared the same father, Terah, but Sarah had a different mother to Abraham. Despite their calling, these two struggled terribly in their marriage, and experienced wider family tensions and splits.

Where we once were in our lives is not what matters, either positively or negatively. We should neither lean on the successes and faith acts of yesteryear, nor be shackled by our failures. What really counts is how we live in response to Christ today.

To ponder: What might you lean on in your past in terms of commitment and faith, and be shackled by in terms of failure?

What really counts is... today

The behind-the-scenes God

FOCUS

'To this he replied: "Brothers and fathers, listen to me! The God of glory appeared to our father Abraham while he was still in Mesopotamia, before he lived in Harran."' (Acts 7:2)

In my early years as a follower of Jesus, I had a rather unhealthy view of the way God interjects with our daily lives. To me, every single event in life had significance and purpose. I tried to trace God's hand behind every incidental happening. I no longer take that view: we live in a fallen world where bad and chaotic things happen, and God doesn't always get His way. That's why we pray, 'Your Kingdom come, Your will be done.' We don't take it for granted.

But I've also overreacted, and failed to see God's hand at work. The great choreographer quietly worked behind the scenes in Abraham's life. Before his father Terah and his family settled in Harran, Abraham had previously received a revelation from the Lord while still living in Ur – Stephen made that clear in his brave final speech before martyrdom. In Ur, Abraham has a revelation of the true God. Then his father makes the decision to move. The text is clear: 'Terah took his son Abram... and together they set out from Ur' (Gen. 11: 31). But later in Genesis, we get God's perspective on that relocation: 'I am the LORD, who brought you out of Ur of the Chaldeans' (Gen. 15:7).

Terah made a choice, probably oblivious to the bigger picture that the God of the universe was quietly at work, and this decision hugely affected Sarah as Abraham's wife. Perhaps there's a deeper, as yet unseen purpose, in being where you are. Behind the decisions that you or others have made, God may have been working to a bigger plan.

God's hand
at work

Prayer: Lead me, Father, and help me to trust You, even when Your work is quiet or hidden. Amen.

Imposter syndrome

Read:
Genesis 11:30
1 Timothy 4:12–14

FOCUS

'Now Sarai was childless because she was not able to conceive.'
(Gen. 11:30)

I t was a surprising yet liberating conversation. Sharing a conference platform with a well-known speaker, he privately shared his experience of self-doubt. 'I often feel like such a fraud,' he mused. 'I'm up there on a platform preaching confidently to tens of thousands of people, but if they knew how I battle with my thought life, struggle with the same sins, and am often plagued with doubt, I wonder if they'd bother to listen to me at all. I feel like a fraud.'

I was heartened by his words, because while we never want to print a licence to sin, we *all* fail. Every Christian can fall into a spiritual form of imposter syndrome, where we fear that if people really knew us, they would reject us.

Sarah was surely a candidate for those feelings. In a culture where being a wife also meant being a mother, women were made to feel they were not 'real' wives if they could not reproduce. Failure to deliver children was the most common cause of divorce in those ancient times. There were further stigmas attached to barrenness, as we'll see tomorrow. For now, let's focus our prayers like this: pray for those in Christian leadership, that they will manage their own fragility and humanity, and perhaps be more honest and vulnerable about it. Leaders should be inspired and challenged by the call to set an example, but being an example is not the same as presenting a false image. Christ lived a sinless life; but never said we, as His followers, would.

Prayer: For those who lead Your people, Lord, may they live lives of clarity, integrity and example. Strengthen them, Father. Amen.

Shame

Read:
Genesis 11:30
1 Peter 2:9–10

FOCUS

'Now Sarai was childless because she was not able to conceive.'
(Gen. 11:30)

Shame is a shroud. Like a suffocating blanket, it weighs heavily, steals our joy, and sends hope packing. To continue our thoughts on her barrenness from yesterday, Sarah's inability to conceive would mean she felt like a 'non-wife', and was heartbroken not to have a child to love and bring up. In her culture, the inability to bear children was seen as a sign of the gods' displeasure. Another strong belief was that a person's offspring would take care of them in the afterlife. But as Sarah and Abraham discover the one true God, as we'll see, they are promised a son and heir, and the beginnings of a whole new nation: the people of God. Yet for many years after that promise was given, no child came: an additional source of hurt, frustration and even shame. Sarah seemed to be the obstacle preventing God's promise from coming to fruition.

Shame is quite different from guilt, which can be a gift: it's good for us to feel guilty when we are. Without guilt, we would have no moral compass. But shame is overwhelming, and often quite irrational. Guilt is targeted. It says, 'You did this, and it was wrong.' Shame writes us off: 'You are wrong.' Perhaps, for whatever reason, you are bound by shame. Others have told you, in no uncertain terms, that you are a failure, with little or no value. Reject shame, and accept God's verdict that you are called, blessed and forgiven. The gospel is wonderful good news. Let's make it the foundation of our lives.

called,
blessed and
forgiven

Prayer: Grant me wisdom to know the difference between shame and guilt, Father, and may I live in Your wonderful grace. Amen.

CWR Ministry Events

Please pray for the team

With the extraordinary circumstances we have needed to adapt to this year, we remain committed to delivering biblically based courses and events that connect you to God, His Word and each other. Whether in person at Waverley Abbey House, or via online platforms enabling you to engage with our training from the comfort and safety of your own home, we trust you will join us and continue to be taught, inspired and encouraged by our programme of events.

For the latest information, please visit our website: **cwr.org.uk/courses** or follow us on Facebook where we will keep you up to date with dates and booking information.

We are still offering a full College programme, and value your ongoing prayers for all our staff and students at Waverley Abbey College as they continue their studies in Counselling and Spiritual Formation.

For further information and a full list of CWR's courses, seminars and events, call **(+44) 01252 784719** or visit **cwr.org.uk/courses**

You can also download our free Prayer Track, which includes weekly prayer points, from **cwr.org.uk/prayertrack**

cwr.org.uk

Barrenness and beginnings

Read:
Genesis 11:30
**2 Corinthians
12:1–10**

FOCUS

*'Now Sarai was
childless because
she was not able
to conceive.'
(Gen. 11:30)*

Before we move on from Sarah's barrenness (although we shall return to it later), I'd like us to notice that, in Genesis, God's activity starts with barrenness: it is the gateway to new beginnings. Right at the start, when the earth was formless and void – barren – God speaks and brings light, life, fruit, flourishing. And now we hear that Sarah was not only barren, but well past the age of childbearing. In other words, Sarah and Abraham are at a place of emptiness and impossibility. But it is to this couple, for whom hopelessness and acceptance of the *status quo* seem inevitable, that God comes with the promise of a child (impossible) and an entire land and a people that will be a blessing to the entire earth – also entirely impossible.

As followers of Jesus, we too are called to a place of emptiness, where we know that for all our human ingenuity, without Jesus we can do nothing. The apostle Paul discovered this to be true. Previously a man in a place of prestige, he'd given all that up, but in the place of nothingness discovered that, 'when I am weak, then I am strong' (2 Cor. 12:10).

As I write this, I am about to preach four times over the coming weekend. Despite studying and working hard to prepare, and after many years of preaching experience, I feel weary and inadequate, and so my prayer throughout today has been a confession of emptiness and an urgent request for God's Spirit to fill me. Like Sarah, I need my inability to be met with God's ability.

**Prayer: Lord, without You, I'm barren. Fill me. Use me.
May my emptiness trigger Your enabling. Amen.**

Called to God's mission

Read:
Genesis 11:31
Philippians 3:7–11

FOCUS

'Terah took his son Abram, his grandson Lot son of Haran, and his daughter-in-law Sarai, the wife of his son Abram, and together they set out from Ur of the Chaldeans to go to Canaan.' (Gen. 11:31)

'I won't be going to the service tonight,' he said. And then, with a smirk, he explained why. 'It's a missionary service. They'll show hundreds of photos of people from Africa – it's so dull.' I was sad, and wanted to say that many missionaries are heroes. Willing to be uprooted and live far from children and grandchildren, they have sensed a radical call from God, which in most cases is incredibly costly.

According to Jewish sources, Sarah married Abraham when she was 15, and he was 25. We know that they were living in the cosmopolitan city of Ur, a humming place with a large population and some beautiful, elaborate buildings. But now, after 50 years of marriage, Sarah would be uprooted from family, friends, from everything that had become familiar to her over five decades. And this was because her husband had received a call from God. Yet we hear no murmur of complaint from her. She was willing to trust that Abraham had truly heard from the Lord, and then lay aside everything she held dear to join him in what appears to be a life of great uncertainty. In a sense, she and Abraham were missionaries, because together they were participating in the great mission of God.

Let's pray today for those who, like Paul, have sacrificed much to respond to the call of God and spread the good news. Ordinary humans like us, they must battle with times of fear, loneliness and doubt, but they have been willing to abandon comfort to embrace calling.

Prayer: Thank You, Father, for those who have sacrificed much to carry the gospel around the world. Bless, strengthen and encourage them. Amen.

the great
mission
of God

Read:
Genesis 11:31
Proverbs 3:5-6

Risk brings fruit

I was in Dublin when I met Gary Davidson. Hailing from Oklahoma, with a southern drawl and cowboy boots, he told me he was a missionary, planting a church in Dublin. I tried not to let my face show my thoughts, because the idea of a chap who looked like a cowboy starting a church in the land of saints seemed ridiculous. I was completely wrong, however. Gary and his wife Wilma were used by God to nurture St Mark's, one of the largest and most healthy churches in Ireland. Like many missionaries, they have paid a high price, but they are fully alive, vibrant people! Gary has faced health challenges throughout his life, and they have spent a lot of time far from home, but they are filled with joy and laughter. Risk and sacrifice has brought fullness, or, as Walter Bruggemann puts it, 'The whole of the Abraham narrative is premised on this seeming contradiction: to stay in safety is to remain barren; to leave in risk is to have hope.'* If God is currently calling you to risk, then step out. When God says go, staying means barrenness of soul, and going means joy.

To ponder: Can you think of a time when taking risks in response to God brought great fruit in your life?

*Walter Bruggemann, *Genesis* (Atlanta, USA: John Knox Press, 1982) p118

step out

Obedience doesn't mean a stress-free life

FOCUS

'So Abram went, as the LORD had told him; and Lot went with him. Abram was seventy-five years old when he set out from Harran. He took his wife Sarai' (Gen. 12:4–5)

Her face was crestfallen. 'I don't understand it, Jeff. When the offer of this new job came up, I did everything I could to consult the Lord. My husband and I fasted and prayed, we shared the details of the new role with our small group, and I felt certain this was a door God was opening. But six months later, I'm wondering if we missed God's will. The company is going through a restructure that is unsettling, and my boss is really difficult. I think we took a wrong turn.'

I've had countless conversations like this, and they are based on this false premise: if I seek God, obey what I sense to be His direction, then things will always go well. It is not always the case. As we saw yesterday, taking risks in obedience to God will ultimately bring good fruit, but there may be stress on the journey. This was a junction moment for Sarah and Abraham. He had clearly heard from God. After some years spent in Harran, now it was time for them to relocate, together with some of the people they had 'acquired' while living there. Some commentators believe that former moon worshippers Abraham and Sarah had been sharing their faith in Harran because the word 'acquired' has overtones of proselytising.

God had clearly directed, but conflict, confusion, bad decisions, family pressures and even dislocation – all that was still ahead. When life is tough, let's not conclude we have missed God's purposes.

Prayer: When I am trying to be faithful, and life brings unexpected challenges, help me to stand firm and trust in You, faithful God. Amen.

Resources for you and your church's wellbeing

After some of the unprecedented challenges faced all over the world this year, perhaps many of us have been reflecting on the meaning and importance of wellbeing, in our lives and in our churches. Now that we are starting to look ahead to another new year, this is a great time to consider how to invest in your walk with God, and in your own spiritual, mental and emotional wellbeing, throughout 2021. God cares deeply for us, and that includes all aspects of our lives.

We have two series that you, your small group or your whole church can engage with to help you live well, place God at the centre, experience His *shalom* peace and goodness and the impact this has on every aspect of our wellbeing.

These Three Things and **God's Plan for Your Wellbeing** are based on sound biblical teaching around how we have been designed to depend on God to meet our every need, and that He longs to meet those needs for us. Each has been developed with an abundance of additional resources available online, including sermon outlines, small group discussion starters and videos, to enable you to really get the best out of the teaching, whether through face-to-face or virtual learning.

These Three Things

Mick Brooks, CWR

God's plan for us is to live in relationship with Him, and look to Him as the primary source of our security, self-worth and significance. Because we are made in His image, only He can satisfy our deepest longings. Through 42 daily readings, explore how we can know life in all its fullness, even when things go wrong.

PROVISIONAL
COVER

God's Plan for Your Wellbeing

Dave Smith, Kingsgate Church

In this brand-new series, created with both Christians and sympathetic enquirers in mind, Dave Smith follows the wellbeing narrative of the Bible, and explores how when we discover God's plan for our wellbeing, we experience fuller understanding of His care and concern for the physical, spiritual, emotional, vocation, relational and financial areas of our lives.

Living with unanswered questions

Read:
Genesis 12:6–10
1 Corinthians 13:12

FOCUS

'Now there was a famine in the land, and Abram went down to Egypt to live there for a while because the famine was severe.'
(Gen. 12:10)

Questions. At the beginning of my journey of faith, I had so many. With virtually no Bible knowledge when I became a Christian, the Bible was totally confusing to me, not least because mine was the King James Version: a rich translation but almost totally incomprehensible to an unchurched 17-year-old. Over the years, I have read, listened, researched, and expanded my understanding. But I rather expected that my questions would decrease. In fact, these days, I have even more. Don't misunderstand: my foundations of faith are secure. Questions remain, however, as so they should, if my faith is expanding.

As Sarah accompanied her husband Abraham to Canaan, they were both motivated by the promise of God, of blessing. A wondrous time was ahead under God's hand. But soon after arriving there, they began to experience precisely the opposite. A severe famine hit, so serious they were forced to temporarily abandon the land that God had promised them, which must have brought turmoil. That surely prompted questions. Were they being disobedient? What had happened to the promise of God? Had they misheard? Blessing and famine don't usually sit together.

Questions are good, because they often lead to understanding. But they can also seem threatening, even paralysing. Some of my questions are being answered: perhaps some never will be. When life seems confusing and even contradictory, we can trust.

Prayer: Help me to use questions to deepen my faith and understanding, Father. Amen.

Suffering because of selfishness

FOCUS

'*Say you are my sister, so that I will be treated well for your sake and my life will be spared because of you.*'
(Gen. 12:13)

Two minutes earlier they were playing together so happily, having fun. But then one of the five-year-olds had held on to one toy that wasn't his for just a little too long, and the juvenile equivalent of World War III broke out. 'It's mine!' was the scream, followed by a punch or two. We don't have to teach children how to be selfish. As human beings, it comes to us naturally.

As Abraham instructed Sarah to play along with his deception that she was his sister rather than his wife, he placed her in danger. She was a beautiful woman, and now she was out there, available to the advances of other men. And if their lies became known (as ultimately, they did) then she could be killed by an angry suitor.

Often fear is fuelled by selfishness. We are so concerned about what will happen to *our* future, *our* stuff, that we allow fear to take root in our lives, and even make decisions that could hurt others in order to protect ourselves. Look at Abraham's language, which is telling: 'so that I will be treated well for your sake and my life will be spared because of you.' It's all *me*.

Perhaps you find yourself in a similar situation. Like Sarah, you have been negatively affected by somebody else's self-centred choices. Yet as we'll see, despite the mess that Abraham made, God remained faithful and helped them through. Even when we suffer because of decisions made by others, God is still faithful and able to help.

Prayer: Save me from the deception of selfishness, Lord. Help me to look to the interests of others, and not just my own. Amen.

God is still faithful

Our not-so-great ideas

FOCUS

'Say you are my sister, so that I will be treated well for your sake and my life will be spared because of you.' (Gen. 12:13)

Scanning Facebook recently, I came across a vitriolic post against Christianity. It was especially heart-breaking because it came from a former worship leader with whom I have shared platforms. He was angry and on the attack, and as I read his bitter words, I wondered how he had made the journey from loving Jesus to rejecting Him. Perhaps it was a series of small steps, a gradual erosion in his faith until finally it had gone.

Some people deliberately decide to march away from God, but surely most drift away gradually. Abraham had begun well, obeying God's call, but then perhaps his hasty retreat to Egypt was a perilous step. We have no record of God sending him there. Once there, Abraham concocts a dangerous scheme that, as we saw yesterday, could have been dangerous for Sarah. Perhaps one small step of independence quickly led to another, and another...

At the moment, I feel I need to be especially diligent in staying close to God, not because I want to be more spiritual, but because I am aware of my own fragility. Some of my best ideas have turned out to be disastrous. I didn't take adequate time to seek the Lord or get good advice. I live with consequences to this day.

God had promised blessing and was working things out for Sarah and Abraham, but Abraham took control back into his own hands. God wants us to stay close. Jesus says that without Him, we can do nothing. We'd do well to believe Him.

without Him, we can do nothing

Prayer: Lord, I'm prone to drift. My confidence can deceive me, so stay close, and help me to stay close to You. Amen.

Be careful who you listen to

As Abraham comes up with his terrible plan to make it appear that Sarah was not his wife, we might ask why on earth would she go along with such a ruse? In a way, poor Sarah had no choice. In the culture of the day, the husband was king. Nevertheless, it's worth taking a close look at the way Abraham spoke to her, because his plan to deceive Pharaoh was more of a command than a suggestion. A close look at the Hebrew text shows that his words were direct and strong, and appealed to logic. Put another way, Sarah heard something like this: 'Look, you know I'm right. This is the only sensible way forward, so just do it.' But the logic was flawed, and the plan would lead to disaster.

From Eden onwards, we humans have been bombarded with ideas that seem true enough, but they are lies. Eve listened to the serpent, and then Adam listened to Eve: and we all know how that turned out. Today, marketeers and advertisers insist we need their products. Hollywood promotes unhealthy and damaging lifestyle choices, and, like sheep, we go along with them, believing the propaganda. And our own hearts, which can be so wicked and deceived, can also lead us astray. Let's be careful which voices we tune in to, and realise, just because the crowd seems to believe an idea, it may not be right. We are called to be non-conformists, not breaking step with everyone else for the sake of it, but willing to do so, if God calls us in a different direction.

Prayer: Fill my heart and mind with Your truth, Your way, Your perspective, Father. Amen.

Read:
Genesis 12:11–13;
3:1–24

FOCUS

'Say you are my sister, so that I will be treated well for your sake and my life will be spared because of you.'
(Gen. 12:13)

Rationalising sin

Sarah is taken into Pharaoh's palace, probably into a harem. She is a victim of trafficking, yet staggeringly, Abraham doesn't lift a finger to help her. One of the most awful scriptural verses follows: '(Pharaoh) treated Abram well for her sake, and Abram acquired sheep and cattle, male and female donkeys, male and female servants, and camels' (Gen. 12:16). Perhaps Abraham rationalised his self-centred behaviour on three fronts. Firstly, he was powerless before the might of the ruler of Egypt, and owning up to the deception might cost them their lives. Secondly, he could tell himself there was some truth in his profession that Sarah was his sister: she was his half-sister. Finally, as he basked in the favours Pharaoh showered upon him, he might even rationalise that Pharaoh was the channel of God's blessing, and this warped arrangement was part of the plan.

Our capacity for self-deception is stunning. When tempted, we squirm, and find it easy to rationalise our behaviour. When we begin to justify ourselves, let's stop, pray and realise what is going on.

To ponder: Is there an area of your life where you are engaging in self-deception? Ask God to show you any blind spots.

let's stop, pray and realise
what is going on

Mind the gap

Read:
Genesis 12:11–16
Ephesians 6:10–17

FOCUS

'And when Pharaoh's
officials saw her,
they praised her to
Pharaoh, and she
was taken into his
palace.' (Gen. 12:15)

Yesterday we considered the awful truth that Abraham apparently did nothing as Sarah was taken into the royal harem. We must wonder how Sarah felt about this, because it's likely that she was now a sexual plaything for the Pharaoh (I don't think that he showered her husband with gifts because of her conversational skills). As we will see, Pharaoh then came under God's judgment for 'taking' Sarah, and it's unlikely that this would have happened had he not had sex – which was adulterous as well as abusive – with her. We are not told how long Sarah suffered in this way, but she was now living in a situation that was directly at odds with what she might have expected, given that her husband had received such amazing promises from God. She was living in the gap between the promise and the fulfilment of that promise.

Many believers are living in that place right now. Holding out for physical healing, they remain sick. Worried about the destructive lifestyles that their prodigals are living, they sense that God has something far better, but in the meantime, the pain continues. And all of us live in the gap between the ascension of Christ and His second coming. One day, everything will be placed under His authority, but in the meantime, we live with His kingdom here but yet not fully here: the tension between the 'now' and 'not yet'. If, like Sarah, you are specifically living in the gap of tough times, hold tight. Hold tight to God.

Prayer: Enable me to stand firm on the evil day, and having done all, stand. In Jesus' name. Amen.

Blessing is not always a blessing

Read:
Genesis 12:16
Matthew 19:16–26

FOCUS

'He treated Abram well for her sake, and Abram acquired sheep and cattle, male and female donkeys, male and female servants, and camels.'
(Gen. 12:16)

As a businessman, he had a terrible reputation. Most of his deals were shady. Whenever his finances went south, he would declare bankruptcy so that he could escape paying creditors, who were owed millions. He operated an 'investment program' that promised much but defrauded many out of millions – some of whom were contacts that he'd cultivated in church. But he kept bouncing back, and insisted that God was blessing and vindicating him. He viewed any and all financial increase as a sign of blessing: an idea prevalent throughout Jewish history that has been popular in some Christian churches. But not all increase is a sign of blessing; on the contrary. Abraham prospered because Pharaoh was so delighted with his new 'acquisition', Sarah. Female donkeys were valued because they were easier to control, and camels were just being introduced as domesticated animals and so were rare. Abraham found himself with the symbols and trappings of prosperity. But his riches were paid for by Sarah, probably every time she had to surrender her body to Pharaoh.

Just because a person is rich doesn't automatically mean that God is blessing them. The gains may have come from unjust or crooked dealings, as here.

Let's ask God to provide for us and bless us as we work hard, be grateful and content when He does, and refuse dishonest gain. And if finances come that are because of God's blessing, let's make sure if we have money, money doesn't have us.

refuse
dishonest
gain

Prayer: Lord, grant me enough, but not too much that might destroy me. Amen.

Spiritual Formation at Waverley Abbey College

'Spiritual Formation has broadened my concept of my heavenly Father, and strengthened my faith by challenging what I believe God is doing in every part of life. God is good, and this course helps us see our spiritual lives more clearly.' – Steve (student)

At Waverley Abbey College, our successful Spiritual Formation programme will soon be entering its third year. From the beginning, we have supported students to reach their full potential, and this year will be no different.

While engaging in knowledge and conceptual frameworks drawn from theology, psychology, social sciences, historical studies, counselling, leadership studies and psychotherapy, students also benefit from time spent in prayer and devotion.

There are many options to learn within the Spiritual Formation programme, with teaching from practitioners and academics in their field of expertise. Options include university validated Higher Education options, as well as single module choices in:

- Mentoring and Coaching
- Chaplaincy
- Pastoral Care
- Spiritual Direction

These are extraordinary times, bringing about an altered pace of life with challenges for many. The need for spiritual guidance continues, and the modules that we teach equip people with the skills and tools to help others grow and develop in their Christian faith.

To find out more, please visit
waverleyabbeycollege.ac.uk/online-open-day

God had to step in

Read:
Genesis 12:11–20
John 14:15–21

....

FOCUS

*'But the LORD
inflicted serious
diseases on Pharaoh
and his household
because of Abram's
wife Sarai.'*
(Gen. 12:17)

I know I'm lingering on this part of Sarah's story, but it's so horrifying, it would be wrong to move on hastily. She must have endured what one writer graphically describes as 'frantic days and sleepless nights' at the harem. Her virtue and dignity were systemically stolen as she became a plaything for Pharaoh. As we've seen, no help came from her husband. Surely she cried out to God during this awful season, and He heard and responded.

Judgment fell on Pharaoh's house. At last he was held responsible for his actions. Those around him suffered too, because the outbreak of serious skin diseases afflicted his household. Some scholars suggest that Sarah was probably unaffected by this sudden plague, which is why Pharaoh knew that the judgment had something to do with her. Bad actions can reap bad consequences.

But let's focus back on Sarah. What might have become of her if God had not directly stepped in? Would her husband have continued to enjoy the high life while she suffered? Sometimes God has to step in and do what we're called to do; perhaps if Abraham had just taken the risk and spoken up, confessing his deception, his wife and others would not have endured such pain.

Sometimes obeying God is very difficult to do. Recently I've found myself in a real battle of the will, wanting to do what's right, but irritated with the cost of doing the right thing. Let's not presume God will step in if it's in our power to act.

sow good
seeds

Prayer: Knowing that what I sow, I will reap, help me to sow good seeds into my life, Lord. Amen.

Beauty for ashes

Sarah was pushed around a lot. We've already seen the forcefulness of her husband's 'suggestion' about deceiving Pharaoh. She was placed in a harem, a frightening situation in which her freedom was a memory. And now, as an irate Pharaoh discovers the deception, Sarah is ejected from Egypt, together with Abraham. The wording used here implies force and rejection. It's a sad portrait of a couple who had received such stunning promises from God. I wonder how Sarah felt, delivered at last from the harem, yet where would they go now? Where is God in all of this terrible mess and upheaval?

But look again. Quietly, behind the scenes, God was redeeming terrible decisions, and setting Sarah and Abraham on a journey that would ultimately lead them to the land of promises, although there would be some further scrapes and mishaps along the way. In life, we often find ourselves in circumstances we would definitely not choose, and we are tempted to feel abandoned by the Lord. But He is able to use even negative 'pushes' by our circumstances to steer us in the right direction. Today, let's not waste time looking over our shoulders, wishing that we could undo yesterday's poor choices, and the choices made by others that have harmed us, as it was in Sarah's case. Rather, let's offer ourselves afresh to the Lord, confident that He can bring order even out of the chaos that we have made. Bringing beauty out of ashes: that's His speciality.

Read:
Genesis 12:17–20
Isaiah 61:1–4

FOCUS

'Then Pharaoh gave orders about Abram to his men, and they sent him on his way, with his wife and everything he had.' (Gen. 12:20)

Prayer: Thank You, loving God, for the grace that gives me peace about my past and hope for my future. Amen.

Visit **cwr.org.uk/podcast** to listen to a podcast

FOCUS

*'Now Sarai, Abram's
wife, had borne him
no children.'*
(Gen. 16:1)

Alone, and perhaps feeling guilty again

Perhaps you know the feeling only too well. You are at a Christian gathering, singing songs about the love of God, but the words you are singing seem distant from your own life. It's not that you don't believe that God loves His world – of that you have no doubt. It's just that it is much tougher to believe God loves *you*, with all your faults, foibles and sins. The preacher delivers a message about God's love, and you feel even more isolated.

Sarah must have been tempted to wonder if she was somehow being judged because of her ongoing inability to conceive. Consider the starkness of this passage, contrasted with the promise of a child to Abraham and Sarah and the fact that no baby was appearing. The reminder that she was Abraham's wife simply underscores the expectation that she should be able to bear him a child, and this must have led her to suffer terrible angst. Infertility was always seen as the woman's problem. God had promised, and now she was the obstacle to the fulfilment of that promise. Ultimately, that turmoil would lead her to come up with a terrible plan, as we will see. When we are insecure about God's staggering love for us, we lose hope, and can drift into some foolish decisions. Today, this very second, you are utterly accepted and loved by God, whatever you may feel. With God's help, believe it.

Prayer: You love and like me, Father. Help me to live in the reality of Your smile over me. Amen.

Read:
Genesis 16:1–2
Psalm 22:1–31

When God doesn't intervene

Two weeks before my father decided to become a follower of Jesus (after decades of having no interest in doing so), the Lord gave me a picture of him with an open Bible in his hand, a tear running down his face. The night after he made his decision to become a Christian, we presented him with a Bible, and a tear ran down his face. God intervened. But there have been other situations where I have longed for something similar to happen in the lives of others I love, but to no avail.

God had intervened in Sarah's husband's life, directing, speaking, delivering. But now, not only had He not yet intervened, enabling Sarah's aging body to bear a child, but He does not speak any caution or command (or none recorded) as she comes up with her own plan to solve the problem of their childlessness. Obviously, He could have spoken. He did speak to Abraham, He would speak later to Hagar, but now, as Sarah comes up with her idea for her husband to sleep with her servant, God is silent. Sometimes God speaks and breaks in, sometimes He doesn't. Again, what is called for is not just faith, but trust.

To ponder: Why is God apparently silent at times?

not just faith, but trust

God's timing

Read:
Genesis 16:1–2
Galatians 6:9–10

FOCUS

'Now Sarai, Abram's wife, had borne him no children.'
(Gen. 16:1)

Let's continue to ponder what it must have felt like for Sarah to know that promises have been made, but there is no sign of them being fulfilled. Sometimes promises and dreams from God simmer in our souls for long periods, and we are tempted to abandon hope. No less than 25 long years would pass between Abraham receiving God's promise and Sarah giving birth to Isaac. I'm reminded of Moses, who spent four decades after his bungled attempt to intervene to help his nation, until God finally called him to lead the people into liberation. Joseph was separated from his (largely) treacherous family for two decades, until the day came when he was in the right place, at the right time, to deliver them, rescuing them from economic disaster. Esther discovered that she had been called 'for such a time as this', but that time only came after 25 years of waiting. And then the man who gave us a third of the New Testament, that amazing church planter and missionary, Paul, spent ten years in total obscurity back in his home city of Tarsus following his conversion and initial meetings with the church in Jerusalem.

When we read Scripture, we can cover hundreds of years when we turn over a page. But when we look closer, we discover that God is not in a hurry, which, frankly, is frustrating – as Sarah found. One African theologian described God as the 'three mile an hour God'. We are called to walk through life, not at our pace, but at His.

not at our pace, but at His

Prayer: I wait for You, Lord. Hear my cry. Amen.

Using God

I can't imagine what Sarah was thinking, or what she felt, as she encouraged her husband to sleep with another woman. She must have been desperate. She came from a background where polygamy was thought of as normal, but what we have here is a mess. She has been used by Pharaoh, and now she commodifies her servant for her husband's use. But Sarah justifies her choice with religious language; seeing her barrenness as the result of God's displeasure (as we've seen, a common idea at the time), she makes her incredible proposal. God's name is used in the same sentence as a suggestion of adultery.

I've been in ministry for four decades, and I've lost count of how many times people have used the name of God to justify plans that obviously were not His will at all. God must get weary of the amount of times that His name is used to support ideas that He opposes. The most extreme example of this was a friend who insisted that God had told Him to abandon his wife and four children so that he could be 'free' to go and plant a church. No amount of pleading and biblical discussion would dissuade him. Unsurprisingly, the church plant was a disaster, a beautiful family abandoned, and the name of God smeared by his behaviour. Let's be very careful before we rush to involve God and claim His endorsement upon what we want to do, especially when it's painfully obvious that our plan is contrary to what He has already stated clearly in His Word.

Prayer: I want to do Your will, Lord, but help me to be thoughtful when I affirm that what I'm doing is what You are directing. Amen.

Read:
**Genesis 16:1–2;
3:1–24**

FOCUS

'so she said to Abram, "The LORD has kept me from having children. Go, sleep with my slave; perhaps I can build a family through her."' (Gen. 16:2)

'Helping' God

Read:
Genesis 16:1–3
Luke 10:38–42

FOCUS

'So after Abram had been living in Canaan ten years, Sarai his wife took her Egyptian slave Hagar and gave her to her husband to be his wife.' (Gen. 16:3)

Sometimes, when I look at my schedule for the forthcoming weeks, I groan. There can be back-to-back meetings, preaching trips, radio programmes to record, study to do for an upcoming sermon series, and a book to write. It all looks intense. I'm not complaining, because ministry is a huge privilege, but asking: how much is God in what I do? It's one thing to be busy, it's another to be preoccupied with projects that God is not really in. Spending ourselves to give to Jesus what He doesn't really want is not a way to live. One of Jesus' friends, Martha, discovered that as she fussed around in the kitchen, feeling resentful towards her sister. She was exhausting herself to give something to Jesus that He didn't see as a priority. Mary had chosen the better way, as she sat at His feet and learnt from Him.

As we consider Sarah's foolhardy plan, we might think that she did this because of her own need to be a mother, and surely that was part of it. But perhaps another reason for her action was that she so wanted to see the promise of God to Abraham fulfilled, and so she initiated this in a misguided attempt to make that happen. Perhaps she believed He needed her to 'help' Him a little, as though He couldn't make it happen. And that can be very dangerous. Let's allow God to do what only He should do, and ask Him to help us in our busyness, not just to bless our activities, but to initiate them.

Prayer: Save me from doing things that You don't want or need me to do, Lord. Amen.

I'm a person, you know

Read:
Genesis 16:1–4
Luke 19:1–10

FOCUS
'Go, sleep with my slave; perhaps I can build a family through her.'
(Gen. 16:2)

It's a question that people sometimes ask me: what should we call you? I'm tempted to say, 'Jeff is my name' (only Kay calls me Jeffrey, and then only when I've done something wrong, which of course happens so infrequently...!). When I'm asked the question, it's usually in connection with what I do as a minister. That's why at Timberline Church in Colorado, where I'm a teaching pastor, most people call me 'Pastor Jeff'. That's kind, and they are showing respect for what I do, but I must confess that I'm most comfortable when I'm simply addressed by my name. It's not just a matter of personal preference. I've come to believe that when others use our names, they are more likely to see us as people, and not commodify us. It's harder to be mean about 'John' than it is to rip 'the vicar' apart with undeserved criticism during Sunday lunch. Notice that in discussing and arguing about their plan, neither Abraham nor Sarah refer to poor Hagar by name: she is totally objectified – a slave. No matter how normal for their time, it still isn't right.

We too can fail to see people. Unique human beings with stories, wounds and flaws pass by us every day, but often we don't notice them as people, especially those of us who work with people a lot of the time. Sarah and Abraham didn't 'see' Hagar. Just as Jesus saw that small tax collector and used his name, today, let's see people. Being noticed is a delight; being overlooked, ignored or commodified is painful.

Prayer: Enable me to notice people today, Lord. Amen.

let's see
people

Joyless sin

FOCUS

'He slept with Hagar, and she conceived.'
(Gen. 16:4)

The announcement in Scripture is blunt and joyless. A baby has arrived, but not in the way God intended, because even though this was the way things were done in ancient times, a person has been used as a commodity, a machine for making babies. As we'll see, there would be other negative results from Sarah's plot. But for now, let's consider how she must have felt. A baby has been born, but this has just confirmed that, medically, it was her infertility and not Abraham's that had meant no child had come from their union. Now there was the sound of a baby crying in the house, but she could never hold that child as her own. Perhaps her mind was also tormented with thoughts of her husband being intimate with another woman.

Here's the truth about what happens when we wander into sinful patterns of behaviour: ultimately there will be no lasting satisfaction or joy. Temptation offers delight, but the excitement of sin will always ultimately be tempered by emptiness and shame. We bite the forbidden fruit, only to discover that it is rotten to the core. There may be a temporary thrill, but it comes with a cost.

When tempted, let's realise that the offer being made to us is laced with lies. Because the enemy is by nature a thief and a robber, not only will he try to steal our integrity, but he will also rob us even of any satisfaction that we might find when we yield to the temptation. Don't be ripped off.

Prayer: Help me to see through the lies of temptation, Father. Help me to walk in Your freedom, and the abundant life You offer. Amen.

Read:
Genesis 16:1–4
Ephesians 6:11

Back to the garden

Let's pause for a moment, because eagle-eyed commentators have noticed a parallel between the journey that Sarah and Abraham took in the Hagar plan with what happened in the temptation experience of the first couple, Adam and Eve, in the garden of Eden. It seems that the story is written to deliberately make a link between Eve's actions and Sarah's. Adam listened to Eve, Abraham listened to Sarah. When we allow the voice of deception to drive us, there will be trouble ahead and, as we've seen (but it's worth repeating), we can be adept at hearing the wrong voices. Then Sarah took Hagar, just as Eve took the fruit. Eve gave the fruit to Adam; Sarah gave Hagar, again, like an object, to Abraham. In both situations, the men knowingly engaged in sin; both were fully responsible for their actions, willingly led astray. Temptation can come in cunning disguises, but they are not original. The enemy of our souls uses familiar tactics, so let's not be ignorant of the devil's wiles. When we can see through his strategy, we are less likely to fall for it.

To ponder: Is there a temptation that keeps emerging in your life, and you have not seen through the strategy and responded accordingly to it?

let's not be ignorant of the devil's wiles

Unexpected consequences

Read:
Genesis 16:1–4
Proverbs 11:18

FOCUS

'When she knew she was pregnant, she began to despise her mistress.' (Gen. 16:4)

I spend part of my time as a certified LifePlan coach, walking people through a two-day, one-to-one process that enables them to chart their journey to date, distilling wisdom from their pathway, which can then help them create vision and strategy for the future. Nobody can 'plan' a life, but we can take a good look at what is and what has been, in order to better navigate what's ahead. My experience as a coach (and in my own life) is that often decisions were taken hurriedly, without careful consideration of the potential consequences, which frequently had a far greater impact than anticipated.

That's exactly what happened for Sarah. In her desire for a child, she must have faced the pain of her husband having sex with another woman. That alone would be difficult. She surely considered that the child would never really be hers, even if she insisted that Hagar, her slave, would play only a minor role in his upbringing. But there was another, perhaps unanticipated consequence of this disastrous arrangement, because Hagar began to 'look down' upon Sarah. We don't know if words were spoken: perhaps it was just a smirk here, a moment of muttering there, but Sarah felt humiliated. When we're about to make an important decision, let's think, pray and ask God to show us what the fruit of our choices might be. And then let's realise that we might not foresee some damaging consequences until it's too late.

Prayer: Grant me a sober heart and mind, Lord, to choose well today, and thus create a better tomorrow. Amen.

Perfect Gifts for Christmas...

Advent

Unexpected Jesus

God's people had been waiting for a Messiah for as long as they could remember, but when He arrived, He wasn't quite what they had expected. Spend each day of Advent reflecting on how Jesus transformed lives in unexpected ways. Ideal for individual or small group use.

By Anna Robbins
ISBN: 978-1-78951-258-8
£6.99

Advent Together

Journey through *Advent Together* as a family, with daily Bible readings, thoughts and activities for the everyone to enjoy. Take a look at Old Testament prophecies about Jesus, and how we can prepare to celebrate His birth.

By Steve and Bekah Legg
ISBN: 978-1-78951-265-6
£8.99

Family Devotionals

More 12-week family devotionals from the Legg family. The four titles can be read in any order.

All Together
ISBN: 978-1-78259-692-9

Time Together
ISBN: 978-1-78259-798-8

Life Together
ISBN: 978-1-78259-999-9

Growing Together
ISBN: 978-1-78951-264-9
£8.99 each

For children and young people

The Camel Who Found Christmas
The littlest camel is concerned about going to see the new king who has been born. However, on the journey he learns from Mama Camel that everyone is big enough, everyone is important enough, everyone is smart enough and everyone is special enough to meet King Jesus.
By Alexa Tewkesbury
ISBN: 978-1-78951-273-1
£1.99

50 Christmasiest Bible Stories
With colourful cartoons and his unique style of storytelling, Andy Robb brings some of the Christmasiest Bible stories to life.
By Andy Robb
ISBN: 978-1-78259-418-5
£5.99

One You, One Year
These one-year devotionals are packed with inspiring Bible readings, relevant thinking points and life changing prayers. Written in an engaging and upbeat style with specific themes, these books will encourage young people in their walk with God.

One You, One Year: 365 for Boys
ISBN: 978-1-78259-994-4

One You, One Year: 365 for Girls
ISBN: 978-1-78259-993-7
£9.99 each

Ideal for ages 10–14

For women and men

Gifts for women

NEW

Unwavering

Jen Baker explores the power of living an intentional life, and how we can make decisions boldly and confidently when we remember who we are in Christ. An encouraging and thought-provoking read for women of all ages.
By Jen Baker
ISBN: 978-1-78951-247-2
£8.99

The Beauty Within

For women of all ages, this interactive, reflective journal considers how God sees us as His daughters, and how we can cultivate an inner beauty that reflects His image.
By Rosalyn Derges
ISBN: 978-1-78259-832-9
£12.99

Gifts for men

The Code

Written by the team at Christian Vision for Men, this is a 12-point honour code for today's Christian man to live by, and respond to the call to live an uncompromised, Jesus-centred life.
By Carl Beech, Nathan Blackaby and Ian Manifold
ISBN: 978-1-78951-149-9
£8.99

Or order by post – see order form on last page

Christian living

NEW

Provisional cover

NEW

Specks and Planks

Jeff Lucas is back with another collection of touching, funny and profound stories from his years of following Jesus. These short but heart-warming anecdotes bring a disarming level of insight to everyday experiences, causing you to ponder, laugh and see life through new eyes.

By Jeff Lucas
ISBN: 978-1-78951-244-1
£8.99

God's Plan for Your Wellbeing

Drawing lessons from the life of Elijah, church leader Dave Smith looks at how we can go back to God's plan for our physical, spiritual, mental, emotional, relational, vocational and financial wellbeing. With additional free material available online, this book makes a great resource for churches and small groups to journey through together.

By Dave Smith
ISBN: 978-1-78951-279-3
£8.99

Multi-buy offers available

Exaggerating the pain

Tension crackles in the household as Hagar, a slave, enjoys a blessing that her mistress does not share. Yet Sarah is guilty of two unhelpful reactions. Firstly, she exaggerates the scale of the problem. The Hebrew word that she uses for 'wrong' means violence. There's no suggestion of that in the narrative. Sometimes conflict is increased when we use inflammatory phrases. If, in marriage or friendship, we rush to preface a complaint with 'You always...' we are asking for trouble!

Sarah totally shifts the blame onto her husband for the tense situation between her and Hagar, conveniently forgetting it was *her* idea that Abraham should sleep with Hagar, so she might conceive. Sarah adds some religiously manipulative language to escalate the conflict as she calls upon the Lord to vindicate her. When we refuse to take responsibility for our part in the erosion of a relationship, and try to win by insisting the problem is not with us at all, we destroy any hope of resolution.

Of course, these truths are difficult to remember (and much harder to apply) when we are embroiled in the heat of conflict. If you're in an ongoing situation of tension and disagreement, perhaps it would be good to step back and calmly consider: am I exaggerating my complaint, and trying to avoid owning my shortcomings? Perhaps it's time to examine our own hearts before we rush to accuse.

Prayer: Lord, may I respond in a measured way when I am hurt. Help me to take responsibility for my own part when conflict erupts. Amen.

**Read:
Genesis 16:4–5
Romans 14:12**

FOCUS

'Then Sarai said to Abram, "You are responsible for the wrong I am suffering. I put my slave in your arms, and now that she knows she is pregnant, she despises me."'
(Gen. 16:5)

step back and calmly consider

The power of hate

Read:
Genesis 16:1–6
1 John 4:7–21

FOCUS

'"Your slave is in your hands," Abram said. "Do with her whatever you think best." Then Sarai ill-treated Hagar; so she fled from her.'
(Gen. 16:6)

Hate is such a powerful force. I know of a family where two siblings have not spoken for years, refuse to go to the same family gatherings, and swat at each other with spiteful exchanges on Facebook. The level of vitriol is stunning, especially as they claim to be Christians, yet are very open about their desire to totally destroy the other. One side insists their campaign is fuelled by a desire for integrity and holiness.

Released by her husband to do as she wished with Hagar (an act of cowardly retreat by Abraham), Sarah turns to spite. One translation says, 'Sarah humiliated her.' The same term is used to describe the extreme suffering endured by the Israelites in Egypt (Gen. 15:13; Exod. 1:12). Some believe Sarah made Hagar work without rest and abused her verbally. Others think violent physical abuse was involved.

Whatever the actual mistreatment was, it was bad enough to make Hagar run away – a desperate measure, for her survival depended on the protection of a family. And as she runs, the writer makes it clear that she is running from Sarah, because the literal Hebrew is 'she ran from Sarah's face'. If you are currently waging a campaign of hate, stop, think – and repent. Remember, you can't love God and hate your brother or sister.

Prayer: Whenever bitterness begins to settle into my heart, may I bring it to You, lest it distil into hatred, loving Father. Amen.

Hagar – known by God

Read:
Genesis 16:7–8
Luke 12:6–7

FOCUS
'And he said, "Hagar, slave of Sarai, where have you come from, and where are you going?"' (Gen. 16:8)

This series of notes is about Sarah, not Hagar. But Hagar's story is intertwined with Sarah's, so let's consider her plight for a few days. A terrified fugitive, probably heading back to her home country of Egypt, she feels abused and threatened. But God knows where to find her, and she meets an angel. I've often wondered how I would react if I bumped into one of those winged warriors – the usual human response is screaming terror. But look closely at this encounter, as the angel gently speaks her name. A woman who has been treated as a commodity is now identified by one of God's messengers. Simply put, God knows and deeply values her. That truth turns her life around and, as we will see, causes her to make the tough decision to go back to serve Sarah.

We live in a fast-paced world where we can feel tiny, insignificant, devalued. The truth that God loves us can lose its lustre because we are so familiar with it. So today, take a few moments to reflect on and celebrate the fact that you are personally known by God – every detail about you, every element of your history, every intricate detail of your character and personality. To God, you are not just a face in a crowd of billions. He knows you and your name. And in that total knowledge, He utterly loves you. Some 'love' is based on *not* knowing the other person, and when the truth comes out, the love fades and ends. But with God, we are utterly known, and still utterly loved. Thank God.

Prayer: You know me, and You completely love me, and I am glad and grateful, Father. Amen.

we are utterly known, and still utterly loved

Hagar – called by name

Read:
Genesis 16:7–8
Isaiah 43:1–7

....

FOCUS

'And he said, "Hagar, slave of Sarai, where have you come from, and where are you going?"' (Gen. 16:8).

One of the most embarrassing moments of my life came when a young man asked for prayer at the end of a service. Introducing himself by name, he shared that he felt so insignificant and unnoticed. 'I go to a party, Jeff, and nobody spends much time talking with me. I'm boring. And nobody ever remembers my name.' It was then that I quietly panicked, because I had not made the effort to store his name in my memory. Now I was going to have to pray for him... and couldn't bear the thought of being yet another person who had forgotten his name, seconds after hearing it.

Before we move on from the moment where Hagar heard her name being spoken, and the sense of value that she must have felt because of it, let's remember the power of using someone's name. Zacchaeus, that infamous tax collector, socially ostracised because he exploited so many, heard Jesus speak his name. Radical transformation followed. Young Samuel heard his name repeatedly whispered through the night, and thought it was Eli, only to discover the calling voice belonged to God. And on resurrection morning, Mary heard her name spoken by someone who she wrongly thought was a gardener – it turned out that He was her Saviour and ours. As we celebrated yesterday that we are known by God, let's recognise the power of using people's names. Earlier we saw that Sarah had treated Hagar as a commodity. But God does not view her like that. Let's bless others by using – and remembering – their names.

Prayer: You know my name, Lord. Thank You. Help me to empower and encourage others as I call them by name. Amen.

Read:
Genesis 16:7–9
Ezekiel 36:26–28

Hagar – change your attitude

I like new things, and fresh opportunities. There have been a number of times in my life when God called us as a family to take steps that, humanly speaking, involved significant risk. I've enjoyed the challenge, although there were some moments of terror along the way. But sometimes just keeping on doing what we're doing, with its challenges and frustrations, can be harder. The grass seems greener and we're tempted to grab the opportunity for change. God's word through the angel to Hagar was a call to return to the difficulties of living as part of Sarah's household. But there *was* to be change – a change in Hagar's attitude. Told to submit to Sarah, the word used implies humility. God has noticed Hagar's difficulties, but He has also noticed her haughty attitude. So now she was called to go back, but to behave differently – a tough challenge. Perhaps we're in a place at the moment where it is tough. We may be more than keen simply to jump ship, but God might be calling instead for a change of heart in us, rather than a change in our circumstances.

To ponder: Is there an attitude change that God is calling you to acknowledge and embrace with His help?

called to... behave differently

You are seen and heard

Read:
Genesis 16:10–14
Hebrews 5:7–10

FOCUS

'You shall name him Ishmael, for the LORD has heard of your misery.'
(Gen. 16:11)

I am currently creating something of a challenge for Kay, my wife. I wear hearing aids, one of which is broken. This means that when Kay speaks, two out of three times, I don't hear her. She's unendingly patient, but I know it must be frustrating to be talking to someone, sensing you are not being heard, even if you repeat what you say a couple of times.

We saw yesterday that Hagar was called to a difficult task, to return to the household where she had been so badly treated. But she is sent with the knowledge that God is with her: He has heard her prayer, and knows of her misery. Strengthened by that comforting word, she embraces the difficulties of obedience.

I find prayer difficult. I used to teach that prayer is a conversation, but I confess that, mostly, it isn't. In prayer, I address someone who is currently invisible. Sometimes He speaks back, but often not; or He speaks, but not immediately, or His voice is unclear. At times, I can be tempted to wonder if I am heard. But that's where faith comes in. The assurance that God hears me and knows me, and my journey is not a matter of feeling, or even experience. You and I are called to ask for God's will to be done, on earth as it is in heaven, even when heaven seems silent. Jesus made His requests in Gethsemane, but didn't receive what He asked for. That doesn't mean that He was not heard, as Hebrews makes clear. Pray today. Your voice, however timid and wavering, will be heard.

Prayer: You hear me, and know every detail of my life and journey, Lord. Help me to live in the good of that truth today. Amen.

God hears

Be who you are

Read:
Genesis 17:1–15
1 Peter 2:4–10

FOCUS

'God also said to Abraham, "As for Sarai your wife, you are no longer to call her Sarai; her name will be Sarah."'
(Gen. 17:15)

Chatting with some friends from New Zealand, I was bemused by the way they pronounced my name. My name is Jeff, but when they say it, the 'e' sounds like an 'i', leaving me with an unfamiliar and unusual name: 'Jiff'. The name is the same, it's just the pronunciation that's changed. Something similar happens with Sarah. 'Sarai' means 'princess'. And Sarah means... you've guessed it: 'princess'. The name has the same meaning, but the pronunciation has changed very slightly.

Name changes in Scripture signify and celebrate defining moments. Peter was once called Simon, but then got a new name that meant 'rock'. Sarah's husband Abraham had a divinely orchestrated name change too, from 'Abram' (high father) to Abraham (father of nations). But for the biblical character Sarah previously known as Sarai, there was no change to the meaning.

I'm speculating here, but is it possible that the 'princess' had always been a princess in God's eyes, had always been the one chosen to be a mother of nations? She was a princess when she was in enforced exile in Egypt, and she was a princess when she was a trafficked person in Pharaoh's harem. She was even a princess when she came up with the disastrous Hagar plan and mistreated her servant so horribly. Now that identity was being clarified and reaffirmed.

God calls us names too in His Word and, just as Sarah was affirmed as royalty, so are we. Today, let's live in that prophetic identity, and live up to our name.

Prayer: Help me to live in my royal identity today, Lord. Show me what that means. Amen.

Visit **cwr.org.uk/ podcast** to listen to a podcast

Blessing for Sarah

Read:
Genesis 17:1–16
Luke 1:39–45

FOCUS

'I will bless her and will surely give you a son by her. I will bless her so that she will be the mother of nations' (Gen. 17:16)

Over the last year, some well-known church leaders have insisted that only men are qualified to serve in Christian leadership and teaching positions. This is not the place (and there is not space) for me to outline the theological reasons why I totally oppose their views, but I do want to make my position plain: I am convinced there is no 'ceiling' created in Scripture to prevent women from serving at every level of leadership. I thank God for His blessing and calling upon so many gifted women. During a recent ministry trip, I spent some time talking with a distraught leader who was bewildered and considering abandoning her leadership role, because of bruising comments, rejecting her leadership because of her gender.

Not only was the news of an elderly woman giving birth shocking to Abraham, but the announcement of God's blessing directly upon Sarah was radical too. Abraham and Sarah lived in a culture where any sense of divine blessing was declared upon the male. Scripture records this pattern too. But now Sarah is not just seen as blessed as a participator in the blessing upon Abraham, but blessed in her own right, although Abraham would obviously need to co-operate in the conception of the child!

As we move forward in this Advent season, we remember another woman who was directly singled out for blessing: Mary. If you are a female leader, I pray that you will be encouraged today to fully pursue your God-given calling.

fully pursue your God-given calling

Prayer: Strengthen and bless all women who faithfully serve You in leadership, Father. Amen.

The hyper-God

Read:
Genesis 17:16–17
Ephesians 3:14–21

FOCUS
'kings of peoples will come from her.'
(Gen. 17:16)

B ecause these notes are prepared quite some time in advance, I am writing this at a time when fears about the coronavirus pandemic are still at a high. To be very honest, right now, the virus seems very big – and God seems small. Crises do that to us; the problems loom large, and our anxieties increase, especially at night, when our capacity for fear is greater. Our vision of God shrinks. Surely years of waiting could have taken a toll on Sarah, but now she receives the stunning news that not only will she have a child, but that she will be a literal princess, as a mother of kings. And ultimately the King of kings would come through her lineage. God's blessing would surpass anything that she might have hoped for in her wildest dreams.

Writing to the church in Ephesus, Paul points them to the superlative power of God, who is able to do 'immeasurably more than we can ask or imagine'. I don't often quote Greek or Hebrew words in these notes, but Paul's language merits a closer look, because in describing God's power, he uses the word *hyperekperissou* (I know, that's a mouthful). We use the word 'hyper' to describe something huge or over the top – a person is hyper, a large store is a hypermarket, and so on. Today, whatever the current challenges, may you know: our God is the hyper God, as Sarah discovered to her joy. The One who called the universe into being with a spoken word. He is our God, a truth not just to be believed, but to be lived by.

Prayer: Increase my vision of You, Father. Lord, increase my faith. Amen.

Sarah's faith celebrated

Read:
Hebrews 11:11
Isaiah 51:1–2

FOCUS

'And by faith even Sarah, who was past childbearing age, was enabled to bear children because she considered him faithful who had made the promise.'
(Heb. 11:11)

God chooses to bless and celebrate some unlikely people, a truth for which we should all be glad. Let's pause for a moment and review what we've seen of Sarah. She could be cruel, jealous and hot-headed. She must have been bruised by some of the mistakes she and Abraham made. She came up with the terrible plan involving Hagar, and then tried to dump all the blame squarely on her husband, even though she had suggested it as a way forward. And as we will see tomorrow, she initially responded to God's promise with a derisory laugh – and then tried to deny that she had reacted that way. She was flawed and imperfect. But then we find her listed in the book of Hebrews' hall of fame, alongside some other unexpected characters, such as Samson, famous for his disastrous dalliances. The prophet Isaiah celebrates her too.

Faith is always imperfect. We can be boldly trusting God one moment, and then wonder if He is even there the next. We need to be more open about our struggles with doubt, not to encourage doubt but to let fellow strugglers know they are not alone. At times, I have found this difficult to do as a Christian leader, as if admitting doubt would be letting the side down. But I think that being an example is not the same as projecting a false image, so I am going to keep on sharing my vulnerability. Let's also know that God loves us and celebrates us, in all our imperfections, our foibles, our sins and our feeble attempts at believing.

Prayer: I am fragile, Father. Strengthen me to trust You today. Amen.

Read:
Genesis 18:1–12
1 Corinthians 7:9

Sarah – blunt about sex

He was quite incensed, and wanted me to know it. I had mentioned sex during a sermon, and it provoked his fury. Storming out of the auditorium, he shouted, 'It's inappropriate to talk about that in the house of God.' He couldn't have been more completely wrong. For one thing, a building is not the house of God: it is just a building. Nor does the Bible shy away from talking very bluntly about sex. Paul's words about it being better 'to marry than burn' are an example. Essentially, he was saying, 'Do you want to have sex? Get married.' Some of the imagery in Song of Songs is so graphic that some commentators and preachers have tried to suggest that it is about Jesus and the Church, unable to cope with the idea that it celebrates erotic love. And as Sarah, who considers herself old and worn out (her words, not mine), hears that she is going to give birth, she wonders to herself how she and old Abraham are once again going to have the pleasure of intercourse. We need to talk more about sex, not less, and bring a biblical perspective in a culture that so misuses this beautiful gift of God.

To ponder: Why do some Christians feel that wholesome talk about sex is inappropriate, when God's Word speaks so plainly about the subject?

beautiful gift of God

Have you always dreamed of visiting the Holy Land?

If so, why not consider joining Jeff and Kay Lucas on an unforgettable pilgrimage next spring? Under their expert guidance and care, they will take you to famous biblical sites, including Galilee, Jerusalem and Bethlehem. Book now and look forward to a well-organised and informative visit. Here's an idea of some of the things you'll experience...

We'll visit some key biblical locations, starting in **Upper Galilee** and the **Jordan Valley**. We'll drive through the **Hula Valley** and along the **Eastern Shore of Galilee**, with a stop at **Bethsaida**, before passing **Jericho** and ascending to **Jerusalem**. No visit to Jerusalem would be complete without a stop at the **Western (Wailing) Wall** and the **Temple Mount**, **St Stephen's Gate**, the **Pool of Bethesda** and the **Via Dolorosa**.

Other highlights will be a visit to the **Mount of Olives**, the **Garden of Gethsemane** and the **Garden Tomb**, where there will be an opportunity for shared Communion. Also, we'll visit **Bethlehem** and view the **Church of the Nativity** and the **Shepherds' Fields**, and have an opportunity to hear about local community work there. We'll travel down the **Jericho Road** to the lowest point on earth at approximately 1,300 feet below sea level, enjoy a visit to **Qumran**, where the Dead Sea Scrolls were found, and then ascend to the **summit of Masada** by cable car to hear its amazing story.

Finally, we will visit the **Israel Museum** to see the Dead Sea Scrolls and the stunning Holyland

Model of Jerusalem, showing the city as it may well have been in the time of Jesus, before a final visit to the **Old City** for some haggling or simple relaxation.

What others had to say about the tour...

'The memories of this tour are priceless. Jeff brings to life the Bible stories in such a way that one can imagine being there in Bible times.'

'Jeff and Kay kept the momentum of the tour consistent, and the amount of places visited in a very safe and organised fashion is truly remarkable – superb!'

'Our Israel trip was both a spiritual journey and an amazing adventure. Jeff and Kay were great hosts. Our tour guides in Israel and Jordan were knowledgeable and fun.'

'The tour schedule was very manageable and allowed for people to see all the sites, wander alone or just rest. Unforgettable holiday!'

Book your place now and join Jeff and Kay from 27 April – 4 May 2021.

For more information, visit **toursforchristians.com**

Sometimes faith seems laughable

FOCUS

*'So Sarah laughed
to herself as she
thought, "After I am
worn out and my
lord is old, will I now
have this pleasure?"'*
(Gen. 18:12)

Perhaps it's happened to you. You are in a social setting with people who don't share your faith, and some philosophical questions about the meaning of life come up. Someone makes a mocking comment about belief in God, and you suddenly feel very foolish. You want to speak up, and it's not that you're afraid to do so – it's just that, at that moment, you are paralysed by uncertainty, and don't know what to say. Or you go to pray, and the idea of God being able to listen to the intercessory murmurings of millions and millions of people seems absurd. Your prayers are brief, dutiful, but not heartfelt.

Sarah had one of those moments, and it seems like it was a snigger of unbelief, not joy. Abraham had fallen over laughing when he heard God's promise, and was not rebuked for it. As we'll see, God gently and tenderly corrects Sarah's giggling.

Once again, we see the humanity of these biblical heroes. Like us, they stagger from great faith and obedience to foolishness and unbelief. It might be that your faith is being tested right now, and you feel ashamed because trusting God seems like a stretch. Growing in faith is not a straightforward uphill trek, always steady and sure-footed. There will be stumbles along the way. The mother of nations, Sarah, had her moments, so perhaps you and I are in good company, especially when we remember again that, in Hebrews, her faith was celebrated and honoured by God.

Prayer: When faith feels foolish, strengthen my heart, Father. Amen.

Own up, there's grace

Sarah laughed, but she laughed to herself, and yet God knew what was going on in her heart. The original language that is used suggests a sense of shock from God, that Sarah would respond to His promise in the way she did. That's not to say He was surprised, but there's an element of dismay and disappointment here. But then Sarah, challenged about her unbelieving attitude, tries to wriggle out of the awkward moment by denying that she had laughed within. Clearly, it was a ridiculous thing to do, because the God who knew what was going on in the inner caverns of her heart would also know she was lying. Pause for a moment and know: God knows our inner thoughts. Nothing is hidden from Him, as John affirmed. Hagar had discovered God could see her; Sarah learned God could see *within* her. That reality should have helped her to realise that if God could instantly know her internal dialogue, He could provide a revival of the marital relationship that would result in the birth of a child. The question is asked, 'Is anything too hard for the Lord?' The timing of the birth is also given, as well as the gender of the baby – it will be a son. Sarah's unbelief and then her attempt at cover-up didn't cancel out the blessing of God.

When we fail, let's not waste time in denial, self-justification, or blame-shifting. Remember, Sarah had done some of that in the Hagar episode. Grace is fully available, and forgiveness is promised as we confess our sins (1 John 1:9).

Prayer: You know my heart, and all my ways, Father. Help me to run to You when I fail, knowing a welcome of grace awaits. Amen.

Read:
Genesis 18:13–15
1 John 3:20

FOCUS

'Sarah was afraid, so she lied and said, "I did not laugh." But he said, "Yes, you did laugh."'
(Gen. 18:15)

God knows our inner thoughts

How to receive news of the impossible

FOCUS

"'How will this be,' Mary asked the angel, "since I am a virgin?"' (Luke 1:34)

As we're thinking about how Sarah received news of God doing the impossible, and this Advent season continues, let's consider how another woman responded to a surprise announcement from heaven.

Mary, the 'highly favoured' one, becomes greatly troubled at Gabriel's announcement: the word used means she began to argue back and forth within herself. Sarah laughs to herself; Mary is in turmoil within. And no wonder, because she was being told of an event that had never happened before in human history: a virgin birth. Then comes the moment when the angel leaves her. She is left alone to deal with the stunning, confusing news. There were complex social issues too – she would have to convince Joseph that no impropriety had taken place, and there was the potential for scandal and danger. While the death penalty for adultery does not seem to have been carried out often in those times, it was still there. There were surely so many questions. But questions and surrender go together. We can be bewildered and obedient at the same time, as Mary was. In the midst of her confusion, she declares that she is the servant of the Lord.

Questions are valued in Scripture, because they are pathways to greater understanding. I don't have to *understand* what God is doing to *submit* to what He is doing. If you find yourself in that place of confusion today, don't wait for clarity before you willingly submit to God. Submit, and perhaps clarity will come.

questions and surrender go together

Prayer: Father God, when I am afraid and confused may I quietly submit to You. Amen.

Here we go again

Read:
Genesis 20:1–7
Proverbs 1:1–33

I mentioned previously that I am writing these notes during the coronavirus lockdown. During this time, I have felt that I've learned some lessons about myself, and have rediscovered what is really important in life. Bombarded daily by terrifying headlines and statistics, I have wished I could go back to the pre-virus days and worry about those smaller issues I was dealing with then – except that I can't remember what some of those issues were right now…

But I am also wondering, will I continue to live in the good of the lessons learnt now, or will I, will we all, just go back to doing life the way we did before?

Incredibly, we see Sarah and Abraham in the same situation they were in, back in Egypt, with the old 'She's not my wife, she's my sister' routine. This time, a man is threatened with severe judgment from God because of the deception. Once again Abraham repeats his mistake, Sarah suffers, now a victim of some manipulation by her husband (we'll look at that in detail tomorrow).

The great lessons of life are too precious to be squandered. When we fail to remember and apply them, we continue in vain, frustrating and damaging circles of destructive behaviour. How often have we made bad choices and felt the sting of our failures, only to drift back into them later, because time has eroded the clarity of the lessons we thought we had learned? Let's live today in the good fruit of the wisdom gained yesterday.

Prayer: Lord, I don't want to keep learning the same lessons, and repeating the same mistakes. Give me clarity in my thinking. Amen.

FOCUS

'For a while he stayed in Gerar and there Abraham said of his wife Sarah, "She is my sister." Then Abimelek king of Gerar sent for Sarah and took her.' (Gen. 20:1–2).

Manipulation and control

Read:
Genesis 20:8–13
2 Timothy 3:6–9

....

FOCUS

'And when God caused me to wander from my father's household, I said to her, "This is how you can show your love to me: everywhere we go, say of me, 'He is my brother.'"'
(Gen. 20:13)

Sadly, it's a commonly used tool in manipulating others: the 'If you really love me, then surely you will do what I'm asking' strategy. The words Abraham used speak of loyalty: 'If you're really with me, then you'll do this for me.' But in his case, the way that he shamelessly defends using Sarah for his own protection is even more nauseating. He blusters on about there being 'no fear of God' in the wider culture, even as his own conduct shows little fear of God. The wording here speaks of moral behaviour rather than just awe or reverence. Then he wants her sympathy, as he says that he will die because of her beauty. There's no mention of the danger to her, being used as she will be. If all of that is not bad enough, he then tries to rationalise his deceptive behaviour with the hollow defence that Sarah is his half-sister. Take a moment to recall how God had spoken to both Abraham and Sarah about the child to come: there the Lord clearly referred to Sarah as 'your wife' as if to underline the precise nature of their relationship.

Sarah was married to a man great in faith, and yet with a huge lack of character: self-centred, unwilling to take full responsibility for his sin, and manipulative. When you're being manipulated, often you will be unaware of it, at least initially. If you're in a friendship, a marriage or a church where bullying, pressure and manipulation are used, may you see through it and respond with courage, clarity and wisdom.

Prayer: Grant me clarity when others would seek to control me, Lord, especially when the manipulation comes in spiritual language. Amen.

Read:
1 Peter 1:3–6
Ephesians 5:21

Trusting God in tough situations

Let's pause today and jump forward into the New Testament and see that Peter celebrated Sarah's faith, in a verse that has often been misunderstood: 'Sarah, who obeyed Abraham and called him her lord'. Men who want to control their wives could use this to call for blanket submission to what they see as their authority. But that's not what is celebrated there; rather, it is that in submitting to Abraham, Sarah was trusting God to take her through some very trying circumstances. Marg Mowczko puts it like this: 'Sarah did not submit simply because Abraham was her master; she submitted because she wanted to protect her husband. Sarah, however, did not always go along with what Abraham wanted. For instance, Sarah wanted to dismiss Hagar and Ishmael, but this idea distressed Abraham. On this occasion, God said to Abraham (literally): "in everything, whatever Sarah says to you, listen to her voice" (Gen. 21:12b). In Genesis 16:2, it says that Abraham (literally) obeyed Sarah's voice.'*

The Bible calls us to mutual submission, not the domination of men over women.

To ponder: What does it mean to have a 'mutually submissive' attitude?

*margmowczko.com/submission-respect-1-peter-3_1-6

mutual submission

What a contrast – Joseph

Read:
Matthew 1:18–25
Romans 4:1–3

FOCUS

'Because Joseph her husband was faithful to the law, and yet did not want to expose her to public disgrace, he had in mind to divorce her quietly.'
(Matt. 1:19)

We've been wrestling with the uncomfortable truth that Abraham shamelessly used Sarah in order to protect himself. If we were in any doubt that God uses highly imperfect people, their story confirms that wonderful truth! Again, as Christmas approaches, it's appropriate to turn to a better example of loving faithfulness and care. Joseph, betrothed to young Mary, is described as a righteous man. The word righteous is also used of Abraham, because he believed God. But Joseph's 'righteousness' was in connection with his behaviour, both towards the law, and towards his fiancée. Initially, he wanted to end their betrothal (and that could only be done by divorce), but he didn't want to shame her, so sought to do so privately.

The beginning of Joseph's story reveals a man who deeply cared about the woman he was betrothed to, and it's a pity that we don't give him more credit. His openness to hearing what God was actually saying, and acting on it, was pivotal. It was his sensitivity to the Holy Spirit, together with his willingness to obey the directions that God gave, that enabled the story to unfold as it did. But let's not overlook his tender concern for Mary. Abraham sadly lacked this concern for his wife, and she suffered because of it. Faith is not just about the way we approach God in believing in Him and His promises, but also the way we treat others – especially, as Joseph experienced, when we are under extreme pressure.

Prayer: Enable me to show my love for You in the loving way that I treat those around me, Father. Amen.

Not shaming

Yesterday, we saw that Joseph refused to take steps that would have left Mary open to disgrace or worse. Returning to the sad, strange story of Sarah and Abimelek, we see a similarity in his attitude to that of Joseph's. As he gives Sarah a very large amount of money, this was more than just compensation for the trying time she had suffered. This was also an act of public vindication for her, a declaration that nothing untoward had taken place between them so that her wider household would not view her with disrespect. When we recall the Hagar incident, and how trouble flared because Sarah's slave took a haughty attitude towards her, this was especially thoughtful, although we don't know if Abimelek was aware of that part of Sarah's history. What is certainly true is that he and Joseph both acted to protect others from shame, and again, this behaviour stands in stark contrast to Abraham's. But let's not be those who relish the failures of others – that kind of gloating is very ugly.

A final postscript before we move on. It was Abraham who prayed, and brought healing to Abimelek's household! God intervenes in this mess. His involvement doesn't imply His endorsement of Abraham's behaviour, but He does respond to his prayers. Next time we hear of a genuine healing through a theologically off-beat and even money-hungry television evangelist, we'd do well to remember that. God blesses messes.

Prayer: You bless me, Lord, with all my frailties and faults. May I weep when others fail, and never rejoice. Amen.

Read:
Genesis 20:9–18
Proverbs 24:17

FOCUS

'To Sarah he said, "I am giving your brother a thousand shekels of silver... to cover the offence against you before all who are with you; you are completely vindicated."'
(Gen. 20:16)

God blesses messes

God is faithful

Read:
Genesis 21:1–5
1 Thessalonians
5:23–24

FOCUS

'Now the LORD was gracious to Sarah as he had said, and the LORD did for Sarah what he had promised.' (Gen. 21:1)

It's a phrase that has become very popular in recent years: fake news. With the access that we all enjoy (or perhaps endure) to instant information through news outlets, the internet and other sources, we are bombarded with information, not all of which is trustworthy. Even a photograph is no longer a guarantee of truth, because every image can be digitally enhanced and altered. We are left unsure of what we should believe.

At last, Sarah gives birth, the one and only 90-year-old to do so in human history. Google states that the oldest mother so far has been Maria del Carmen Bousada de Lara, aged 66 years 358 days when she gave birth to twins. They exclude Sarah, which is a shame, because she holds the world record! As joy comes to Sarah, the Bible is careful to point repeatedly to the faithfulness of God as the cause of her joy. Three times in two verses it is made clear: God keeps His promises, He is utterly trustworthy. That doesn't mean that we are assured of getting anything we want, but when God pledges something, He always follows through.

Our response to that truth should be to commit to reading, imbibing, meditating on and applying God's Word in our lives because it is completely dependable truth. And if you know for sure that God has made a promise to you (not always easy to discern), it will come to pass. Sarah discovered that, even though the waiting had been so difficult.

Prayer: Your Word is a light to me, Your promises create a strong foundation for me to stand upon, loving God. Amen.

Visit **cwr.org.uk/ podcast** to listen to a podcast

It's a New Dawn

Encountering God presents an opportunity for new life and a new start. In the next issue of *Life Every Day*, we'll begin the New Year by looking at what the Bible has to say about our new life, and meet some people who discovered not just a new phase, chapter, or even purpose and mission, but a totally new life of hope and change. For them it truly was a new dawn.

WRITTEN BY
JEFF LUCAS
JAN/FEB 2021

Life Every Day

It's a New Dawn

Applying the Bible to life

CWR

Also available as eBook/eSubscription

Obtain your copy from CWR or a Christian bookshop.

Please note: from the next issue, the price of your copy will be £3.49.

For updated subscription prices, please see the order form at the back of these notes.

God is mindful of us

Read:
Luke 1: 46–56
1 Peter 5:7

FOCUS

'My soul glorifies the Lord and my spirit rejoices in God my Saviour, for he has been mindful of the humble state of his servant.'
(Luke 1:46–48)

As we have followed Sarah's story, we have realised the truth that, when it comes to God, we are always seen by Him. Distraught fugitive Hagar was stunned to discover she was known, heard and seen by God. As we saw yesterday, Sarah experienced the faithfulness of God as the promise of a son was fulfilled. Both she and her husband discovered the impossible is possible, when God says it will happen.

On this Christmas Eve, we turn again to Mary. She too had a revelation of the faithfulness of the Lord, as she heard, ' For no word from God will ever fail' (Luke 1:37). And in her wonderful song that we know as the Magnificat, she celebrated the truth of God's 'mindfulness' of her. 'Mindfulness' is a popular word of late, and it is defined as 'the quality of being present and fully engaged with whatever we're doing at the moment'. The word that Mary uses speaks of God looking at her with tender care. Mary was thrilled, not only by the stunning miracle that God was working through her, but because of God's heart towards her. And in her song, she also celebrates God's help and mercy towards Abraham and so, by inference, towards Sarah too.

Some of us are thrilled that Christmas is almost here. Others approach this time with dread, because we feel alone, there are empty seats at our table, or we have memories of better Christmases in the past. Whatever your situation, may you know strength and comfort as you affirm by faith: God has me on His mind.

Prayer: I am always on Your mind. Thank You, Father, in Jesus' name. Amen.

Breaking the silence

Read:
Luke 2:1–21
Genesis 21:1–5

Imagine the delight of it: the sound of a crying baby, this time Sarah's, the silence of childlessness broken for her after so many years. And on this day of days, when we celebrate the birth of another child, we realise that the 400-year silence that had followed the words of the prophet Malachi (broken only briefly by the voice of John the Baptist), was broken too. The angels couldn't contain their joy, and the night sky had been filled with their music. Shepherds were invited to abandon the fields for a while, to witness the coming of this Jesus. Simeon and Anna added their voices to confirm the uniqueness of this miracle child.

Sarah and Abraham experienced the stunning provision of God enabling a geriatric couple to become parents, and creating a lineage that would lead to the birth of a people, Israel, with royalty emerging from that line. And young Mary and Joseph, a couple just starting out in life, discovered the wonder of a child conceived without human seed, the one who would live and die and rise again to create a new people, a new priesthood, a new royalty, with Himself as their King of kings. Isaac was the child promised in the covenant with Abraham; Jesus came as the child promised by multiple prophets, the light of the world that shines in the darkness.

Today, let's give thanks, because we are not alone, and the God who is faithful has done great things for us. Let's be glad – and have a wonderful Christmas Day!

Prayer: You came for us, Emmanuel, God with us! I worship You, Lord Jesus. Amen.

FOCUS

'While they were there, the time came for the baby to be born, and she gave birth to her firstborn, a son. She wrapped him in cloths and placed him in a manger'
(Luke 2:6–7)

we are not alone

Read:
Genesis 21:6–7
Psalm 30:1–5

God has the last laugh

I love the sound of laughter. Humour has always been a part of my ministry. Whether through preaching or writing, I try to deliver truth with a smile. Humour can be a dynamic tool for teaching, because we laugh when we've understood. And then there is something beautiful about a congregation laughing together.

Laughter had been a feature of Sarah and Abraham's story. Abraham had 'fallen face down' with laughter at the thought of his elderly wife becoming a mother – incredulous laughter. Sarah had laughed to herself when she heard news of a child – laughter that had a hint of unbelief. God has the last laugh, and Isaac – the name commanded for the boy – is a permanent reminder that God is able to give each of us laughter, bubbling up when we experience His care in our lives. Sarah celebrates because she knows that her story – an old lady becoming a mother – will bring joy to everyone who hears it. This weekend I pray that you will hear something in your homes, families or churches that will cause laughter to well up.

To ponder: Has God ever done something for you that caused you to laugh?

laughing together

You could be right

As we near the end of our study of Sarah's life, let's recall some of the negative episodes. Sarah was cruel and spiteful to her slave, Hagar. She suggests an immoral liaison between Abraham and Hagar in a futile attempt to resolve the issue of an heir. She sniggers at God's promise. She tries to shift the blame onto her husband for what was her idea. And Abraham has some truly dubious episodes too, twice endangering his wife in the 'she is my sister' strategy, gladly profiting from her being taken by other men. He uses manipulation to get what he wants. There are other moments too – yet notice Scripture praises both of them for their faith and faithfulness.

As Sarah expressed her frustration with Hagar (again), Abraham was surely tempted to dismiss her complaint, not least because he loved Ishmael. The last time he had heeded advice from Sarah, it had led to disaster, so he could have written her off as unwise and hot-headed. But it turns out that, even in the midst of the domestic stress, God's will was being worked out, and Abraham was instructed to listen to and obey the voice of his wife. Be careful about swiftly categorising people – 'He's just a fool', 'She's always untrustworthy'. Because someone failed yesterday doesn't mean that they are doomed always to be a failure. Jesus ate with sinners – but the Pharisees just labelled them as sinners. And thank God, because He does not define us by our worst moments.

Prayer: Lord, You see more than my failures, You see me. Help me to do the same to others, especially when they have failed. Amen.

Read:
Genesis 21:8–14
Luke 15:1–2

FOCUS

'But God said to him, "Do not be so distressed about the boy and your slave woman. Listen to whatever Sarah tells you, because it is through Isaac that your offspring will be reckoned."'
(Gen. 21:12)

Be gracious – but beware too

Read:
Genesis 21:8–14
Psalm 121:1–8

FOCUS

'But Sarah saw that the son whom Hagar the Egyptian had borne to Abraham was mocking, and she said to Abraham, "Get rid of that slave woman and her son"' (Gen. 21:9–10)

Yesterday we saw there is a danger in labelling people because of their failures, and writing them off permanently. But as a pastor, I feel compelled to issue a word of caution before we move on. Sometimes the Church has been guilty of not providing sufficient protection (for children, for example) from people who have displayed predatorial behaviour. Someone comes into the church who has a criminal record, and the church moves to ensure that this person is not allowed access to those who might become victims. Limits are placed upon their involvement in church life. It's then that someone loudly complains that we are not showing grace and forgiveness, nor offering full trust. And that's a mistake. Grace and forgiveness don't cancel out the need for caution and responsible protective safeguarding.

Another example is the heart-breaking number of cases where Christian leaders have been accused of abusive behaviour over years or even decades, but nobody believed the victims or, worse still, their complaints were covered up. In a desire not to categorise people and show grace, we could place others in danger. Perhaps it's a stretch, but I notice that one reason for Hagar's dismissal from Sarah's household was that she was back to her old mocking ways again, and Sarah was just not willing to allow that pattern of behaviour to continue.

Let's be gracious, cautious and careful too, lest we expose the innocent to unnecessary danger.

let's be
gracious,
cautious
and careful

Prayer: Lord, let those who lead Your people be full of grace, and full of wisdom too. Amen.

Isaac and the sacrifice

Read:
Genesis 22:1–19
Romans 15:5–6

FOCUS

'Then God said, "Take your son, your only son, whom you love – Isaac – and go to the region of Moriah. Sacrifice him there as a burnt offering on a mountain that I will show you."'
(Gen. 22:2)

Occasionally in *Life Every Day* I have had to confess that I disliked the story we were studying together, and this is my least favourite episode in the entire Bible: the call to Abraham to sacrifice Isaac. It is horrifying, and rightly so, because the entire Old Testament is completely opposed to child sacrifice. There's tenderness here, however, amidst the awful demand, as God affirms that Isaac is Abraham's much-loved only son. Perhaps God took Abraham through this to show once and for all that human sacrifice is never His agenda.

But because our reflections are about Sarah, let's focus on the fact that she does not appear in this episode. There seems to be no discussion between Abraham and Sarah about his intentions, which presents many questions. How could he consider such a thing without telling his wife, and if Isaac had died at his hand, how could he ever have broken the news to her?

When we look beyond the Bible, there are various Jewish traditions about this awful episode, including the idea that Abraham did tell Sarah about what he was going to do. There is even a tradition that she died of a broken heart because of the episode. The suggestion is that although Isaac returned safe and well with his father, the trauma of it all was just too much to bear for Sarah. Once again, we're reminded that walking with God doesn't spare us pain, and may actually involve more pain, if we determine to be faithful and obedient to Him.

Prayer: I am under no illusions, Father. Following You surely involves cost. Help me to be faithful. Amen.

Until the end

Read:
Genesis 23:1–20
1 Thessalonians
4:13–18

FOCUS

'Sarah lived to be a hundred and twenty-seven years old. She died at Kiriath Arba… in the land of Canaan, and Abraham went to mourn for Sarah and to weep over her.' (Gen. 23:1–2)

I've already mentioned that I have been writing these notes during the coronavirus pandemic. I have no idea how all this is going to turn out, but it looks likely that many of us could suffer economically, and some will have lost loved ones to this awful outbreak. Walking a life of faith does not mean that we are spared loss, grief, seasons of sadness and questioning. Along with times of sunshine, there are times when the clouds come rolling in, and no amount of faith will spare us from them.

As we end our look at Sarah's life, we see that Abraham had been through many experiences with her – she was an amazing partner. And now, as she dies, he is overwhelmed with sadness, and goes out of his way to honour her memory. I've heard of Christians who have been told not to grieve when a partner dies, because that person is now with the Lord. But we *do* grieve, because they are not here, with us. Our grief is tempered, though, because we have hope.

Like me, like you, Sarah was flawed. She experienced bruising trials. There were many years of frustration, together with the laughter and exhilaration of seeing the impossible come to pass. I've been encouraged as I've reflected upon her life, and I hope you have too. As we stand on the brink of a New Year, let's determine to stay faithful and in faith, right until the end, as she did. God bless you, and thank you, as always, for joining me.

stay faithful
and in faith

Prayer: May I be found faithful as a follower of Yours, all the way until You come or call, living, loving Lord Jesus. Amen.

Order form

5 Easy Ways To Order

1. Phone in your credit card order: **01252 784700** (Mon–Fri, 9.30am – 4.30pm)
2. Visit our online store at **cwr.org.uk/store**
3. Send this form together with your payment to: **CWR, Waverley Abbey House, Waverley Lane, Farnham, Surrey GU9 8EP**
4. Visit a Christian bookshop
5. For Australia and New Zealand visit KI Entertainment **cwr4u.net.au**

For a list of our National Distributors, who supply countries outside the UK, visit cwr.org.uk/distributors

Your Details (required for orders and donations)

Full Name:	CWR ID No. (if known):
Home Address:	
	Postcode:
Telephone No. (for queries):	Email:

Publications

TITLE	QTY	PRICE	TOTAL
		Total Publications	

UK P&P: up to £24.99 = **£2.99**; £25.00 and over = **FREE**

Elsewhere P&P: up to £10 = **£4.95**; £10.01 – £50 = **£6.95**; £50.01 – £99.99 = **£10**; £100 and over = **£30**

Total Publications and P&P (please allow 14 days for delivery)	**A**	

Subscriptions* (non direct debit)

	QTY	PRICE (including P&P)			TOTAL
		UK	Europe	Elsewhere	
Every Day with Jesus (1yr, 6 issues)		£17.95	£22.50	Please contact nearest National Distributor or CWR direct	
Large Print *Every Day with Jesus* (1yr, 6 issues)		£17.95	£22.50		
Inspiring Women Every Day (1yr, 6 issues)		£17.95	£22.50		
Life Every Day (Jeff Lucas) (1yr, 6 issues)		£17.95	£22.50		
YP's: 11–14s (1yr, 6 issues)		£17.95	£22.50		
Topz: 7–11s (1yr, 6 issues)		£17.95	£22.50		
Total Subscriptions (subscription prices already include postage and packing)				**B**	

*Only use this section for subscriptions paid for by credit/debit card or cheque. For Direct Debit subscriptions see overleaf.

All CWR adult Bible reading notes are also available in **eBook** and **email subscription** format. Visit **cwr.org.uk** for further information.

Please circle which issue you would like your subscription to commence from:

JAN/FEB MAR/APR MAY/JUN JUL/AUG SEP/OCT NOV/DEC

How would you like to hear from us?

We would love to keep you up to date on all aspects of the CWR ministry, including; new publications, events & courses as well as how you can support us.

Continued overleaf >>

If you **DO** want to hear from us on email, please tick here [ ]

If you **DO NOT** want us to contact you by post, please tick here [ ]

You can update your preferences at any time by contacting our customer services team on 01252 784 700. You can view our privacy policy online at cwr.org.uk

Payment Details

☐ I enclose a cheque/PO made payable to CWR for the amount of: **£** _____

☐ Please charge my credit/debit card.

Cardholder's Name (IN BLOCK CAPITALS) _____

Card No. ☐☐☐☐ ☐☐☐☐ ☐☐☐☐ ☐☐☐☐ ☐☐☐

Expires End ☐☐☐☐   Security Code ☐☐☐

Gift to CWR ☐ Please send me an acknowledgement of my gift   **C** ☐

Gift Aid (your home address required, see overleaf)

giftaid it I am a UK taxpayer and want CWR to reclaim the tax on all my donations for the four years prior to this year **and on** all donations I make from the date of this Gift Aid declaration until further notice.*

Taxpayer's Full Name (in BLOCK CAPITALS) _____

Signature _____   Date _____

*I am a UK taxpayer and understand that if I pay less Income Tax and/or Capital Gains Tax than the amount of Gift Aid claimed on all my donations in that tax year it is my responsibility to pay any difference.

GRAND TOTAL (Total of A, B & C) ☐

Subscriptions by Direct Debit (UK bank account holders only)

One-year subscriptions (6 issues a year) cost £17.95 and include UK delivery. Please tick relevant boxes and fill in the form below.

☐ *Every Day with Jesus*
☐ Large Print *Every Day with Jesus*
☐ *Inspiring Women Every Day*

☐ *Life Every Day* (Jeff Lucas)
☐ *YP's*: 11–14s
☐ *Topz*: 7–11s

Issue to commence from
☐ Jan/Feb   ☐ May/Jun   ☐ Sep/Oct
☐ Mar/Apr   ☐ Jul/Aug   ☐ Nov/Dec

CWR Instruction to your Bank or Building Society to pay by Direct Debit

Please fill in the form and send to: CWR, Waverley Abbey House,
Waverley Lane, Farnham, Surrey GU9 8EP

Name and full postal address of your Bank or Building Society

To: The Manager _____ **Bank/Building Society**

Address _____
_____
_____
                              Postcode _____

Name(s) of Account Holder(s)
_____

Branch Sort Code
☐☐ ☐☐ ☐☐

Bank/Building Society Account Number
☐☐☐☐☐☐☐☐

DIRECT Debit

Originator's Identification Number

4	2	0	4	8	7

Reference
☐☐☐☐☐☐☐☐☐☐☐☐☐☐☐☐☐☐

Instruction to your Bank or Building Society
Please pay CWR Direct Debits from the account detailed in this Instruction subject to the safeguards assured by the Direct Debit Guarantee.
I understand that this Instruction may remain with CWR and, if so, details will be passed electronically to my Bank/Building Society.

Signature(s)
_____
_____

Date
_____

Banks and Building Societies may not accept Direct Debit Instructions for some types of account